Photo Editing in Photoshop: A Beginner's Guide to Making Pictures Perfect Using Photoshop

Disclaimer and Terms of Use: Effort has been made to ensure that the information in this book is accurate and complete, however, the author and the publisher do not warrant the accuracy of the information, text and graphics contained within the book due to the rapidly changing nature of science, research, known and unknown facts and internet. The Author and the publisher do not hold any responsibility for errors, omissions or contrary interpretation of the subject matter herein. This book is presented solely for motivational and informational purposes only.

Table of Contents

Introduction:

Adobe Photoshop has redefined the way we edit photographs. In the beginning, when there was no photo editing tool, we used to print photos the way they were clicked. Over the years, however different tools have been developed by which one can edit photos. But these tools were available with the professional photographers only. However when Adobe launched their range of photo editing tools, they named it Photoshop. This software was created with the aim to make photo editing easy for the regular photographers like us. This software aimed to bring photo editing within the easy grip of the commoners who did not own a high end camera and the other accessories for clicking sharp edged pictures.

In this book, we will guide and assist you regarding how to use this software to your advantage. Starting from handling the tool box, to the different layers, photo editing, digital art, typography – you will get a detailed account of how to handle and use the software.

Each one of us uses a smart phone and all of us have an account in fb and twitter where we constantly upload images on the go. Some photos just come great and you don't have to do any editing while there are some that are blurry or has got a red eye. If you have Photoshop downloaded in your phone then you can edit it immediately before you go ahead and upload. What is the end result? You get crystal clear images that look like the original and no one will be able to pinpoint that the image has been edited. In this book we will discuss in detail:

- Part 1: The Toolbox
- Part 2: Basic Panels
- Part 3: Introduction to Layers
- Part 4: Basic Menus
- Part 5: Beginner Photo Editing
- Part 6: Digital Art
- Part 7: Design and Typography
- Part 8: Filters

Many users who have not used this software so far might wonder why this software has a cult following across the globe. A powerful image editing software created by Adobe, this software was launched in the year 1990 and since them it occupies the numero UNO position in the photo editing software department.

For a simpler, easy way to edit your pictures Adobe Photoshop is a must. Save money, time and worry be learning how to use this software. Over the years different versions have released. The latest version that you will find in the market is cs6. Both professionals and regular users cannot do without this software.

Clicking a photograph with a high end camera is not enough. Nor the absence of a high end camera can distort the images that you have clicked. Yes, it will lack the sharpness and edge of the photographs clicked with a high end camera with its high end lenses but if you use Adobe Photoshop you can turn a dull dry image into a happening one.

The different tools, panels and the editing techniques will provide you with ample options on how you can edit any image. Once you complete the whole book and start practicing what you have learnt on Adobe Photoshop you will be amazed at the way you can easily edit an image and give it a completely new look. Dull and boring images will become a problem of the past.

For a career in this field or for your personal use, read through the different chapters to grasp the subject in detail. This book will change your concept regarding this software. Go ahead, get going

Part 1: The Toolbox

Adobe Photoshop is one of the most interesting software's to work with. Once you know which tool is used for which function you will be able to edit your own photos. You won't require a professional to edit your pictures anymore. And in the end you will be able to save your hard earned money and time both. So let us get started.

Starting your Custom Workspace:

Once you install this software you would like to play around a bit so that you get a hang of how the software works. Move around your palettes and panels and create different images that you can save in your "Workspaces." This can prove to be quite helpful as you might want to save different images. The CS6 auto saves your changes to your workspaces. So you can create as many images as you want and you can play around before you decide which one to use as per your requirement.

Click the >> to open up the contextual menu. Create a new workspace and save it in any name that you want. You can use your name as well to save the image. In the different chapters we will also introduce you to the different shortcuts that you need to learn so that once you have grasped the subject you can easily shift to the shortcut keys to get your word done.

The Toolbox:

You will get all the different tools that you need to edit an image in the tool box. You can use your mouse or the cursor based tools in order to use them. The tool box is located on the left hand side of the screen. When you click on the ▶▶▬▬ arrow you can come across the condensed version of the toolbox in your panel. The tool box hosts a variety of options that you can use as per your need and specifications. What are the different tools? Let's look around:

- **The Options Palette:** If you look at the top of the screen, right below the options, you will find the options palette. Once you select the different tools you will come across the different edit options. From here you can pick the tool that you need.

- **Rectangular Marquee Tool**: this tool also known as the "Marching Ants" allows you to select the different layers or the flattened photographs (whichever you have in mind). If you press shift +m you will be able to navigate through the different selection tools. If you hold the shift then you can create squares using this marquee tool. Shortcut key for this tool is "M"

- **Move Tool**: this is the basic tool through which you can move around the selected area. You can also move around an entire layer with this tool. Shortcut key for this tool is "V".

- **Lasso Tool**: this is another selection tool by which you can select an area of the image that you would like to get rid of. If you press shift + L then you can use the other two varieties of this tool the Polygonal Lasso and Magnetic Lasso tools. Shortcut key for this tool is "L".

- **Quick Selection Tool**: this tool works like a toothbrush and once you select the area it will get rid of the portion. When you press shift +w you will be able to use the magic wand tool to select the area. Bucket Fill or Flood style tool are the two varieties available. Shortcut key for this tool is "W".

- **Crop Tool**: You can use this tool to create rectangular selections of the portion that you want to highlight. The software will select the portion that you would like to highlight and will get rid of the rest. If you want to create multiple images then press shift +C in order to select the Slice Tool. This tool is generally used for creating web content. Shortcut key for this tool is "C".

- **Eyedropper Tool**: When you are suing this tool you can select a color from any of the documents is open. You can use the other varieties of this tool by pressing shift + I. Shortcut key for this tool is "I".

- **Healing brush:** if you want to get rid of scratches, unwanted marks and blemishes then this tool is the one that you should use. When you press shift +J you can choose between Healing Brush, Patch Tool, and Red Eye tools. Shortcut key for this tool is "J".

- **Brush Tool**: to use this tool, rely on your mouse. Paint with the left mouse clicks and in order to select the different varieties depend on the right mouse clicks. In order to browse through the different brush tools like the Pencil, Color Replacement Tool, and Mixer Brushes press shift +B. Shortcut key for this tool is "B".

- **Clone Stamp Tool**: with this tool you can create a clone of the image that you would like to replicate. Shift +S will give you the pattern stamp tool. Shortcut key for this tool is "S".

- **Eraser Tool**: with this tool you can practically erase the background layers to transparency level. Shift + E will help you select between the different varieties. Shortcut key for this tool is "E".

- **Gradient Tool**: if you want to use this tool then you need to click and drag the tool in order to select the option where you would like to apply this feature. You will find a host of gradients under the options palette. Once you have selected the portion opt for paint bucket tool in order to color the particular area. Shift +G will give you a tour of the different features located under it. Shortcut key for this tool is "G".

- **Blur, Sharpen, and Smudge Tools**: as is evident from the name these tools function as per their name. There is no shortcut key for this tool.

- **Dodge and Burn Tools**: with this tool you don't dodge the image, don't get fooled by the name. On the contrary this tool will help you to darken or lighten the image as per your specifications. Shortcut key for this tool is "O".

- **Pen Tool**: this tool is a bit difficult for the beginners. It is best to avoid this tool unless you want to work with it. Like a pen this tool will help you to select the portion that you would like to edit. Shortcut key for this tool is "P".

- **Type Tool**: this tool will help you type the text of your choice. The moment you use this tool a new layer will be automatically created. In other words you don't need to open a new layer in order to use it. Shortcut key for this tool is "T". We have dealt with topic in detail in the 7th chapter.

- **Path Selection and Direct Selection Tools**: opt for this tool only when you are interested to master the pen tool otherwise it is better to avoid this tool. Shortcut key for this tool is "A".

These tools will help you to draw a direction either in a direct way or through segments.

- **Custom Shape Tool**: this tool will help you to create custom shapes like rectangle, polygons, and lines just like the clip art. Shortcut key for this tool is "U".

- **Zoom Tool**: with this tool you can zoom in or zoom out of the image. Shortcut key for this tool is "Z"

- **Hand Tool**: You can easily scroll down your image with the help of this tool. Press the space to use this tool and once the work is done release the space bar. Shortcut key for this tool is "H".

- **Foreground Background colors**: these colors refer to the default color that is there when you open a new layer. Generally black and white are the default colors. You can always change the colors if you want.

Part 2: Panels

One of the biggest advantages of Adobe Photoshop is also its major drawback. There are so many different options that you are bound to get spoilt for choices. Go through this chapter in order to have a clear idea about the different panels.

Adjusting Panels:

The default panels are located on the right side of the personal computer. They are the perfect tool to begin with as you can easily adjust them, show them, and hide them – as per your requirements. There is hardly anything called the perfect way in Photoshop. It is more about comfort and usability. I case you cannot find the panels you can always search for them in the workspace area of the menu bar. You will find an option that says "reset" and from there you will easily find the adjustment panels.

Exploring Default Panels:

When you open the panels you will see that the "essential" panel is also the default one.

- **Mini Bridge**: built on the similar lines like Google Picasa, this panel will help you browse through the different images located in the different files and folders of your personal computer. This bridge functions in the same way as Picasa although if compared Picasa is a better one.

Through this visual browsing feature you can easily navigate through different files and folders and add them to favorites as well for easy recall later on. Once you select the image that you would like to load, double click it on mini bridge or you can press the right click and select it after opening the image.

- **History:** one of the best features of Adobe Photoshop is this history panel. You can reverse the editing done so far and as many times as you want. As a result you get the opportunity to edit the images in a more natural way. With this panel you can easily revert the editing steps taken so far. In fact you have a better control over your editing.

- **Color**: a simple but interesting panel you can easily pick and choose the colors that you want for your foreground and background layers. You can vary the value from 0 to 255.

- **Swatches**: this is a good resource especially for beginners like you because Adobe Photoshop come pre-loaded with 122 colors from which you can select the colors that you would like to use. Opt for a different color by simply clicking on the new swatch option.

- **Styles**: you can easily opt for the different styles of layers in order to edit the image that you have selected. It is an interesting tool liked by both the beginners and the veterans.

- As a panel of saved "Layer Effects," styles can be an interesting way for beginners to start experimenting or veterans to save their most common layer effects for reuse. Once you select the style it will automatically get applied on the open layer. If you wish you can edit it manually as well. Some of the default panels may appear strange and weird while others may have limited use. There are many who will leave you confused as ever. And yes it is true that all of them are not useful.

Adjustments:

With the adjustment panel you can change and filter the image the way you want it. When you opt for the contrast or hue or saturation panels, the changes made will be permanent. The adjustment panel makes new layers on top of the image that you are editing and you can the adjustment tool inside this panel. And the adjustments that you make can be changed or reversed without using the history channel.

When you opt for multiple adjustment layers, you can stack them one above the other and can edit them even after saving the editing done.

Masks: with this palette you can block out parts of the layers that you want to edit by reducing the transparency level. This is an effective and easy way to remove the background without editing the image in a destructive way.

Layers: with the layers panel you can create 2D images in multiple editable parts. You can easily use the different tools in different layers without affecting the previous or the next layer. All the work that is done in Adobe Photoshop is done in the different layers only. Without the different required layers, the editing is not possible.

Channels: here you will get colors in digital variety and each one of them has separate values that can be increased or decreased as per your requirement.

In order to master Adobe Photoshop there is no alternative to practice. In the next few chapters you will understand why it is extremely important to practice if you want to edit your images without the help of any professional.

Part 3: Layers

One of the foundation pillars of Adobe Photoshop is the layers. They are the techniques of learning good photo editing techniques. The layer is one of the most important panels on which you need to work and when you are using Photoshop you will need to spend ample time on it.

In case you have somehow lost the layers panel you can get it back by going to Windows and then layers. You can create any shape in the layer by using the lasso tool. However this tool does not create a new layer although you can use the selection to move around in the particular layer.

You can create the new layers by clicking on the new layer button in the layers panel. The shortcut key for this step is Control Shift N and a new layer will be opened.

These new layers will be stacked one upon the other just like new images. By default, each new layer is transparent in nature.

You can move, rotate or transform each of the individual layers as per your need. Rotating one layer will not affect the work done in the other layers. After you have edited an image you might want something in the background and you might think that one of the layers will make the image look complete if put at the background so you can easily click on the layer and select the option in order to move it at the back.

If you wish to drag images from an open file to the one you are working on you can use the move tool to do the needful. Photoshop will create a new layer in your required file with the dragged image on it.

In case you want to insert a text on the image, opt for the shortcut key "T" and a new text layer will be created here you can type the text you want. This change will be done without affecting the other existing layers.

With the "blending options" you can easily blend in the images without any difficulty. When you opt for the blending options you will be taken to the layer style panel from where you can take your pick of shadow style, text font and size, style. You can also add a soft glow – all of which are editable.

You can use your adjustment panel to create a "photo filter" so that you can easily lend a sepia tone to your image. With the "gradient" panel you can also add a new dimension to the layer. These layers are great as they can be easily edited and adjusted as per your requirement. There are different types of gradients, colors, angles from which you can take your pick. You can edit or hide the adjustment panel as per your need by double clicking on the layers panel.

When you learn how to use the different layers to your advantage you will be able to use the Photoshop and its different effects to create the type of image you have in mind

Part 4: Basic Menus

Adobe Photoshop is loaded with a host of features that will make your photo editing experience a memorable one. In this chapter we will give you an idea of the different features and how you can use them to edit the image.

The Top Menu:

The File Menu:

In the file menu you will get the common things like the "Open" and "Close" feature along with a host of options like the following:

- **Browse in Bridge**: very similar to Google's Picasa, bridge is a visual browsing feature. Through this you can check out the different images saved in their library rather than empty filenames.

- **Browse in Mini Bridge**: mini bridge is a smaller version of bridge and is installed within the Photoshop but takes quite a lot of time to get loaded.

- **Open As**: once you click on this feature, you can take your call regarding the format in which you would like to open the image. JPEG, bitmap and so on.

- **Open as Smart Object**: when you opt for this feature you can easily resize the image and wrap it from the original file. So if you want to resize an image you can easily open it in Smart Object.

- **Share my Screen and Create New Review**: this feature allows you to register your copy of Photoshop and create your account with Adobe.com

- **Device Central**: you can create a separate program for smart phone users with this feature. However for a beginner it is not that useful.

- **Save for Web and Devices**: with this program you can easily compress your files and store them in different formats like JPG, GIF, PNG, or WBMP file formats. Here the word devices refer to smart phones only.

- **Revert**: with this feature you can reload your file from the time your image was last saved after editing. Often you might end up losing important editing work done if you have not saved it. Still this feature is quite useful.

- **Place:** you can easily insert another file into the one that you are currently using. You can save the image as a smart object.

- **Automate and Scripts**: these features are great especially for the advanced designer who has to do a lot of repetitive work. Even the beginners are going to benefit from this feature.

The Edit Menu:

The next important menu is the edit menu through which you can edit the image in any which way you want. Following are the different features, slotted under it:

- **Undo, Step Forward, Step Backward:** this is a simple and easy way to change your last action. If you want to undo the last step that you took in editing the image then opt for control +Z. this is perhaps the most common way of undoing the previous action. With the forward and backward step you can change the history as well.

- **Cut, Copy, and Copy Merged**: Cut, copy and paste is very similar to all the other software's that you have used so far. With copy merged feature you can copy the multi layer document as if they were merged from the beginning only.

- **Fill**: this is an excellent feature as you can use it to select a particular portion or area that you would like to fill with the foreground or background color.

- **Stroke**: you can create a linear stroke with this tool. Once you select the area with this tool it will color that particular area with a single line. Say for example you want to highlight the borders of the image. Use this tool to draw a linear line against the border. Select the color and the border will be collected accordingly.

- **Content Aware Scale**: it uses the same technology as in content aware fill. Once you resize the image, Photoshop will adjust so that you image looks the best.

- **Puppet Warp**: you can wrap the image in a number of complex ways with this tool.

- **Transform and Free Transform:** with this tool you can practically resize an image, correct the perspective and even distort the image.

- **Keyboard shortcuts**: this is an invaluable asset for any Photoshop user.

- **Menus**: one can edit the existing menus, hide features that they hardly use and highlight the one that they use always.

The Image Menu

With the image menu you can change the color depth and do a variety of other thins to make the image attractive.

- **Mode**: the color mode is the feature by which you select the RGB or CMYK mode or any other color mode that you are interested in. It is better to save the image into RGB unless you are interested to learn the different formats.

- **Adjustments**: here you will find other features stored under the adjustment tool. Some of the commonly used features are brightness and contrast, levels, curves as well as hue or saturation.

- **Brightness/Contrast**: with this tool you can easily adjust the color and lights including the contrasts as well.

- **Levels**: the perfect way to adjust the value range of your photographs.
- **Curves**: with this tool you can adjust the value and the channel with greater accuracy.
- **Exposure**: perfect for adjusting light and contrast.
- **Hue/Saturation**: decide on the brightness or vividness of the color that you would like on your image.

- **Invert**: you are changing the colors in the opposite direction i.e. black will turn white and white will turn black.
- **Posterize**: limit the number of colors for your image with this tool.
- **Threshold**: you can convert your black images to white without the hint of any grey color.
- **Auto Tone, Auto Contrast, and Auto Color**: Photoshop will automatically adjust the tone, color and contrast.
- **Image Size**: you can increase or decrease the image size of the entire image. Don't confuse it with the canvas image.
- **Canvas Size**: it will increase the file's space without altering any of the image information.
- **Image Rotation**: you can easily rotate the image in any direction.
- **Duplicate**: create another file that is identical to the one that is already open. But keep in mind that the new file does not retain any of the editing history.

The Layer Menu:

The basic for editing the different layers used in editing the image, the layer menu has a host of different features loaded in it.

- **New**: with this tool you can easily create new layers. In fact you can also turn the existing layer into a background one. You can group the different layers just like the way we group different files under a folder.

- **Duplicate Layer**: you can easily create a duplicate of the file that you are working on with this tool.
- **New Fill Layer/New Adjustment Layer**: you can easily edit the layer with the fill tool or the adjustment tool by changing the numerical value. You can do it more than once.

- **Layer Mask/Vector Mask**: they are effective in hiding part or all of the active layers.

- **Clipping Masks**: this mask helps to clip a layer or a series of layers to the transparent layer below it.

- **Group Layers/Hide Layers:** you can group several layers as well as hide layer by using these two tools.

- **Align/Distribute**: with this tool you will be able to arrange the layers into your working space.

- **Merge Down**: you can merge the current layer or the other layers with the one below it.

- **Merge Visible/Flatten Image**: with these tools you can combine all the layers. When you opt for the merge tool it will ignore all the hidden layers while the flatten tool will create a non transparent background layer out of all the layered information that you have saved so far.

Other Important Menus:

The following menus are the easy ones. They are relatively less complex and you can work with them in an easy manner.

The Select Menu: here you can use the tools like Marquee, Lasso, and Wand tools, Quick Mask, Modify and so on. In the select menu you can practically select, deselect, and invert any of the work done here.

The Filters Menu: with this tool you can practically give your new edge and dimension to the image. Some of the filters are highly useful while others are hardly used. As per your requirement you can pick and choose and apply the different filters.

The View Menu: as is evident from the name you can view practically almost everything that you have done with the image. You can zoom in and out of the image, change the shape and size of the image, check out the pixel rate and even get rid of the slices or guides if you don't like them.

The Window Menu: this is where you will find all that you have deleted including the options panel and the toolbox.

The Help Menu: this tool will give you an idea of the different tools that are there in the Adobe Photoshop.

In case you have any difficulty in understanding any tool, you can check out this feature to clear your concepts.

Part 5: Beginner Photo Editing

One of the major reasons why Adobe Photoshop is named Photoshop is because you get to edit images in a simple and easy way. In this chapter we will be discussing some of the basic photo editing techniques by using which you can give a new life to the old photos stuck in the photo album. Over the years these photos have remained stuck in the album and the lack of care has left these photos yellowed and discolored. Click a picture of the different photos with your digital camera, transfer it in your personal camera and let's get started. Some of the common things that you need to know as a beginner are mentioned below:

Cropping Images for Better Composition:

Often it happens that after taking a picture, we notice that there are a lot of things in the background that we don't want. One of the best ways to get rid of the unwanted background is through the crop tool. You can use this tool to crop the image to the exact size that you want.

Press the C key on your keyboard and drag the crop tool. With the help of the mouse, drag the crop tool on the photograph. Select the portion that you would like to keep. The rest of the portion will get cropped. In case you want to undo the portion that you have cropped, use the control +Z key to undo the cropped portion.

Adjusting Contrast with the Levels Tool:

You must have noticed that when you click images on a gloomy day, the picture quality is not great. The image appears to be dull and dark, devoid of any detail. You can use a high end camera with a high end lens to solve the problem. But what if you don't own one and it is not possible for you to invest in such equipment. You use a normal digital camera with which you have clicked the image. Use Photoshop to give life to the image. With the adjustment tool you can practically adjust the brightness, color, contrast, clarity and even opt for auto fix to give the image the required effect.

With your image in front of you, press control + L to open the levels dialog box. There you will get the three sliders that represent Shadows, Mid-tones, and Highlights. When you adjust these tools as per your requirement you will get the desired image. Once you have selected the specifications, click on OK to apply them. Immediately you will see a better, brighter and vivid image in front of you. You will be amazed at the naturalist and flawless image in front of you.

Adjusting Color-Shifted Lighting:

One of the most common problems that you will face when you click images at your home is that the colors will be tinted. Indoor lighting is very different from outdoor lighting and it has shades of yellow, red and blue. These shades are normally not visible to the naked eye but our camera tends to detect these colors and as a result they get reflected in the image. If you want to get rid of these then you need to opt for the color shifted lighting tool. How to go about it?

Select Image – Adjustments and – selective color.

Selective color is an interesting tool that allows you to change the primary colors of your images. Red, green and blue are the primary colors while the remaining are secondary colors.

Check your image to see which is the prominent color? If red is the prominent shade then opt for red from the colors menu and then adjust the level so that the impact of the color is reduced.

Sharpen Blurry Photographs without Damaging Color:

Often it happens that an image clicked indoors appears to be blurry and fudged due to the poor indoor lighting. This takes away the magic of the image leaving behind a dull and boring photo that hardly ahs any volume. Unfortunately this blurry image is a problem and you have to get rid of it if you want to improve the quality of the image. So how do you go about it? There are many Photoshop filters that you can opt for that will improve the overall quality of the image. But if you are not wise in your selection your image will get distorted and the color will look patched. However the step we are recommending here is relatively easy and safe for the quality of your image.

Opt for Lab color to give your picture its life. Generally this tool is not frequently used and may not be recommended by professionals but it is the safest way to opt for an alternate color.

In order to switch on to this tab, go to Image click mode, select Lab color as mentioned. When you opt for the shift to the CMYK you will notice a change in the color but not in the Lab color. Your RGB colored image remains same without any kind of color shift.

Now go to your Channels panel. In case you cannot locate it, you can always access it by going to your menu and from there select windows and then channels. Select the lightness channel. This channel will look something like the grayscale version of your image. In case the grayscale version does not get selected, you need to try this step again. (Keep in mind that this grayscale version is very important if we want this tip to work.)

Now go to filters, select sharpen and from there select unsharp mask. This mask filter can be quite harsh and can turn your image quite dark. So you need to select the right level value in order to counter the harshness of the filter. Don't forget to adjust the Midtones and Highlights if you want to retain the natural look of the image.

In case you want to undo the edits, you can go to image and then mode and from there select the RGB mode and save it to JPEG version. It is always a good habit to save multiple versions of your original image so that in case you are not happy you can easily undo the photo editing changes made.

With the different photo editing tools, you will be able to change a regular image into your desired one. The photo editing tools are very simple and easy to follow. It will require a little bit of practicing from your end if you want to grasp this chapter. Once you start practicing use the shortcut keys in order to get the work done in a fast and effective way. We have mentioned all the shortcut keys in the previous chapters. Make a list of these shortcut keys and keep it in front of you for a ready reference. As a beginner, you must do this thing. With several weeks of practice you will know the shortcut keys by heart and then you won't require the list any more.

In these five chapters, we have discussed in detail all the tools, panels, layer and editing tools so that by the time you begin your sixth chapter you have got a grasp of the basic guidelines. Make it a habit to practice what you have learnt after the end of every chapter so that the transition is smooth. If you plan to practice the third chapter first after reading through the first two chapters you will end up in a mess. Photoshop is not that easy until and unless it has been practiced several times.

Part 6: Digital Art

For readers with an artistic bent of mind, we have included this chapter on Digital Art. There are very few photo manipulation software's that will allow you to give wings to your artistic side as the Photoshop. It is the best things to have happened in the world of photo editing. When you want to use your artistic bent for a living or purely for the fun part, Photoshop is equally rewarding.

Getting Started With the Brush Tool:

The brush tool or the shortcut key B is "THE" tool of Photoshop. But it is the most complex of all the tools out there especially with regard to its use. You will get a variety of options with this tool and it is better to get acquainted with all the aspects. In case you cannot locate the brush panel, then go to window and select the brush panel.

Do I Need a Graphics Tablet?

While they are not an absolute necessity but it is true that the use of a Graphics Tablet will improve your Photoshop experience to a great deal. If you search the market you will come across several varieties. Some are very expensive while others are quite affordable. As per your budget select the one that you would like to purchase.

Photoshop has many brush features that cannot be used without a pressure sensitive tablet. You will not only get the option to draw with a stylus but the sensivity of the tablet will also be not there.

Learning the Brush Tool:

Press the control +N key to create a new file. Read through the steps carefully to get a better understanding of this brush tool. Now that you have a new file in front of you, right click on your mouse to open up the contextual brush menu and from there select the first standard brush i.e. the "soft round" brush and select a color say black and create a stroke on the new file. If you want you can adjust the size with the help of the top slider. Now go to your opacity panel and move the slider to 50% mark, once done you will be able to see the difference. The black color will become a bit translucent.

Now once again click on the brush tool to select another variety of brush the "hard round". Keep the opacity as the previous one. Now notice the difference between the two images. The hardness of the brush which ranges from 0 to 100% affects the blurriness of the line that you have drawn.

You can change the intensity of the color by adjusting the "flow" as well. Change the value of the flow to 50% and notice the difference. Zoom in the image for a better understanding.

There is another feature the "Airbrush Mode" that can be very confusing. Nearly every version of Adobe Photoshop has this. Click on the brush style to know the difference. After you have selected the brush style, click and drag your mouse. You will notice that there is a stream of color pigment on the area where you have dragged the mouse. If you stop clicking and dragging the mouse, the color pigmentation will stop! In fact you will notice that the color has been spilled from the area where the brush has been stroked which is very different from the previous two brush experiences. It is best to avoid this brush style unless you are very confident. We have discussed it here because it is better to know the difference between the different types of brushes.

Drawing with Pressure Sensitivity:

Now let us shift our attention to the pressure sensivity feature to experience the difference. Go to the far right side of the tablet and select the "Tablet pressure controls size" located on the top panel. When you use this pressure sensivity with a brush, it line begins small but then grows slowly and is dark throughout.

When you opt for the "Tablet pressure controls opacity," you will get lighter shades with your chosen brush because the opacity level has been decreased. If you opt for the first row of "basic" brushes for this sensivity test you will get interesting results for sure.

Some of the results are weird and unexpected and in certain cases the brushes react in an unexpected way. While there are others that create nice, soft strokes that look natural. When you change the opacity levels, the results will vary.

In addition to these you can also select the direction of the brush stroke.

Digital Inking and Painting with Photoshop

Rather than scanning, it is better if you opt for digital images when you are trying out digital inking and painting with Photoshop. So let us learn how to use the different brushes when you are opting for digital inking. Once you select the image where you would like to learn, go to the image option; select the image size in order to adjust the dimensions. 300 pixels per inch is a standard option. If you opt to increase the width by 10 inches you will create an image that is 3000 pixel wide. If you are comfortable with it then stick to it or select a resolution that works the best for you.

Opt for a solid color adjustment for your photograph. You can opt for any color although through your experiments you will notice that the light colors work the best for this step.

Let us select any color, say pink then opt for the blending mode selected on top of the Screen. You will notice that your image has toned down and you can start your inking process.

Now create a new layer and select the brush tool or the pencil tool in order to ink your image.

Create a new layer on top to draw your ink lines in. Select the Brush tool or the Pencil tool to ink your image. Since you are opting for pressure sensivity your inking experience will become easy and quick.

In order to add color to the image, create a new layer by pressing control shift +N and then create a new group. Remember to create this group under the digital ink layer.

You can fill the image with colors of your choice when you opt for the bucket fill brush. If you want to add multiple layers then opt for "All Layers" on the right side of the options. You can add new layers for each of the different color or can add the different colors in a single layer. As you are looking for a clean painting opt for tinting in order to give the image a clean look.

Digital Art is a great way to give your image a different look. If you want to create a painted version of your selected image then you can easily achieve it with the help of Photoshop. It is a quick and easy way and once you learn to use the different tools you will be able to edit the images just the way you want it.

Part 7: Design and Typography

Adobe Photoshop has opened up new avenues and channels for the would be designers who want to create a life out of their creative skills. In this design and typography chapter we will teach you how to use the type character panel and the design tool in order to edit your pictures just the way you want it.

Fonts and the Character Panel

Although Adobe has other programs like the Adobe Illustrator for handling typography and its different aspects, yet we cannot undermine the role played by Photoshop. With this software you can opt for any typographic features that you will get with the Illustrator.

You can locate the character panel by going to the window panel and then select the character, in case you cannot find it on the right side of the panel. This panel has a host of features that you can use in order to give your text a different dimension altogether. However keep in mind that this panel has certain features whose name is such that it might be a bit difficult to remember. So make a list of the terms and go through it whenever possible so that you have the terms on your fingertips when you get down to work.

- **Font Family:** this tool deals with the type of the font that you would like to deal with. The font family deals with the different varieties like Helvetica, Arial, and Times New Roman and so on.

- **Font Style**: this deals with the style in which the font will be written. Here you can change the different styles like the Arial Bold, Arial Narrow, Arial Condensed, Arial Rounded MT, Arial Black, italics and so on.

- **Font Size**: here you can practically decide on the size of the font. There are certain in built sizes from which you can take your pick. 2, 4, 6, 8, 10 and so on.

- **Leading**: this is a term that is used to define the space between the paragraph texts. You can set the lines in points with the help of this tool.

- **Kerning**: this deals with the horizontal spacing between the different pair of letters. If you want to increase the space then you have to opt for positive numbers and in case you want to decrease the space then opt for negative numbers.

- **Tracking**: very similar to kerning, here you can select the space between letters, if you wish to.

- **Vertical Scale**: with this way you can control the width of the text by squashing it up and down. Once you set the numbers, the text will be squashed accordingly.

- **Baseline Shift**: it is the line on which the text rests. You can move the texts higher or below the baseline by shifting their position.
- **Text Color**: you can adjust the color of the text with the help of this tool.

- **Language**: you can change the language of the text in case you want to opt for a non-English word.

- **Anti-Aliasing:** you can blur the edges of the text with the help of this tool. Once you use this tool you can practically soften the borders of the text.

Faux Bold and Other Character Panel Options

The Options Panel and the Type Tool

There are certain options that are not included in the Character Panel but you can easily access them by searching for them in the Options Panel when you are using the Text and Type Tool.

Designing a Simple Book Cover

In the world of designing, it is very important to know how to design a book cover. This is one of the most common techniques that you need to learn. So let us begin:

Press control +N in order to bring up the level tool so that you can adjust the image of the book cover. Keep in mind that designing a book cover is not merely about the arrangement of elements. Now that the image on the cover has turned black, click on the control key so as to select the gray channel in your channels panel. This will result in selecting the "white" areas in the image. In case your image is not set in the grayscale but is in the RGB or CYMK then you need to go to image and then select mode and from there opt for grayscale before you go ahead and control click on the grayscale channel.

Now press control + shift + N in order to create a new layer. Now go to edit, opt for the fill tool and fill the selected area with white. You will notice that the image has been moved from the black background and can be used as an element.

Now press control +N in order to create a new document in your chosen size. Now select a foreground color in your toolbox. You can opt for any color as per your choice.

Now go to edit, fill the foreground with your chosen color. In the same way select the background color.

Once the color is changed press the shortcut key V in order to navigate your original file. Now move this file into the new file with the help of the move tool.

In order to set the text opt for T i.e. the Type tool in order to write the text. Select the font shape, size, style according to the image and the book cover design you have in mind. Keep in mind that all types of font will not go. So be wise in your selection. Once you have selected the font adjusting it is a very simple affair. Keep a track that leading, kerning, tracking, baseline shift, text color, vertical scale, language and anti aliasing are all in order. A little bit of ignorance on your part and the entire effort will be marred.

Although most of us assume that designing is more about images and photo editing but the text has an important role to play. If the text selected is not appropriate then the entire editing work will be wasted. The end result will be zilch. Don't go by the style that you like but the style that will do justice to the overall editing. In case you think that opting for the italics or bold will add value to the text then only opt for it. Just because you have these features does not mean that you will apply them anywhere and everywhere. Initially you might face difficulty in making the right selection. But with practice you will be able to gauge which text font and style will go. If adding the text color will do justice then only change the color. Adobe Photoshop is all about practice. No one has been able to muster it in a single day. So give time but be dedicated in your approach.

Part 8: Filters

Our last chapter is on filters – one of the most popular topics of Adobe Photoshop. If you can use filters in the right way then you can easily create fun, interesting and memorable photographs. Read on to learn how.

The Big Box of Crayons:

You can easily get tempted by the variety of options that you can use to filter your images. Playing with filters can be fun provided you know how to use them to your benefit. Just because there are so many different options out there don't apply all of them you need to know what you are looking for and the kind of effect you are trying to achieve and accordingly you need to take your call. In fact the different features are so naturalistic that when you apply them no one will be able to make out that the image has been photo shopped. In order to get into the groove, experiment with different filters on a daily basis. After a short span of time you will get the hang of it.

How to filter your images?

Photoshop filters work on the concept that it will help you to filter out all those areas that you don't want to keep in your image. Often it happens that after clicking an image we find that that are certain portions that is affecting the overall image. You can neither crop it because the end result will not be good. So what do you do? You filter it. It is that simple! Filters are basically processing programs that process the selected image in several ways.

What Can Filters do?

For this you need to know what the different types of filters out there are.

Go to filters select artistic and then color pencil. This tool will help you draw colored lines.

Now from filters select cutout. With this tool you can cut out the portion that you would like to get rid of.

Select watercolor from filters. With this tool you will get the exact effect as you get from using water colors on paper. It is so natural.

There are different tools that will help you to blur the portions of the image that you would like to fade out from the image. You can take your pick from Gassian Blur, Motion Blur, Radial Blur, and Smart Blur.

If you want to sharp the dull edges then select brush strokes and from there opt for accented edges, it will give a sharp edge to selected portion.

Some other popular tools include:

- Filter > Pixelate > Color Halftone
- Filter > Pixelate > Crystalize
- Filter > Pixelate > Mosaic
- Filter > Pixelate > Pointilize

All these different pixilated features will help you to add a mosaic look, crystallize look, color halftone impact or pointilize look as per your requirement and specification.

There are some other tools as well that you can opt for. They include:

Pinch, Shear, Spherize (under distort), Add Noise, Reduce Noise (under noise), Clouds, Difference Clouds, Lens Flare (under render), Unsharp Mask (under sharpen), Bas Relief, Reticulation, Graphic Pen (under sketch), Extrude, Find Edges (under stylize), Patchwork, Stained Glass, Texturizer (under texture), Maximum and Minimum (under other).

Combining Filters for Better Results

As with all the other tools and features of Adobe Photoshop, discussed so far in all the previous chapters, you can use the different features of filter in a single image only when you are sure that the final copy of the image will be exactly what you want. If the different filters are combined artfully then the outcome is really impressive. And as we all know by now, a skilled adobe Photoshop user is one who knows which tool to use in order to get the desired effect.

Quick and Dirty Vintage Photo Effect in Photoshop:

Another interesting feature of this filter tool is its capacity of turning a latest picture into a convincing part of vintage art. There are many types of software out there that will give you this effect but the final copy is not that polished nor does it look that genuine. The kind of vintage art created by these software's is unexciting, unconvincing results. But with Adobe Photoshop you can practically and easily turn the latest image into a vintage image.

You can use any image of your preference but make sure that is one with high resolution and with good contrasts between light and shade. The change in the image will be more prominent and it will easier to notice the difference.

So let's get started. Press control shift +U in order to desaturate the image so that it turns into grayscale. Now press control +U so that the hue/saturation palette is opened. From there select the colorize option. Now go to blur (under filter) and select Gaussian blur and select the radius to 1.0. If you want you can opt for a higher range as well. You will see that the image has a sepia tone to it. Now, press control shift +N in order to create a new document. Fill the newly created layer with black. If you want a cloudy effect you can opt for the clouds located under render in the filter section.

Now set your layer effect to screen in the layer palette so that the image fits the screen. Go to opacity and decrease it by 50%. Don't forget to create a duplicate image. (Right click and select duplicate to create the replicated image.)

If you are looking for a monochromatic effect, go to noise (located under filter) and add noise to bring about the change. When you opt for this feature it will give a harsh look to the image. So let is learn how to soften the effect. Opt for Gaussian blur. And voila you will notice the difference.

If you want to adjust your image a bit more than opt for the adjustment layer and select the value in order to tone up the image. You can increase or decrease the opacity, sharpen your image through unsharp mask and so on.

Now to give this image an authentic look, go to the layers palette and adjust the layers again. Adjust the hue or saturation as per your requirement and the final look you want to portray.

Conclusion:

In this book "**Beginner Guide for photo editing in Photoshop"** we have extensively dealt with the different topics in a lucid language so that you get the whole concept at one go. The different tools, features and their application have been described in detail for a better understanding of the topic.

Adobe Photoshop is not a new concept. This photo editing tool was launched in the early 90's and over the years several different versions has been launched. Do not get confused by these different versions. All these versions are a step ahead then the previous one. Some of the tools have become more refined with many more extra features while some have remained the same.

Photoshop as you know it by now is a photo editing tool that can easily turn any faded, dull, boring or distorted image into a proper one. As you go through the 8 chapters you will understand how to handle the different tools and how each one of them will help you to achieve the desired result. However there are two things that you need to do. One is practice. There is no alternative to practice. The more you practice the more skilled you will get in this software. Don't forget to use the different shortcut keys mentioned in the different chapters. Make a list of these shortcut keys and learn them by heart so that you know how to use them to achieve what you want. And the second and the most important thing is don't get tempted by the different tools and their features. Just because you have access to so many different options that does not mean that you need to apply all of them. Using each and every one of the tools will distort the image that you are interested in editing. You need to be clear about what you would like to do with the image and then proceed accordingly.

Adobe Photoshop is a wonder tool. The more you work with this software the more you will be amazed at the different ways in which you can improve the image. Learn to apply the different tools. Keep in mind that most of the steps can be reverted before you save the final edited image so don't hesitate to experiment. The more you are open to experimentation the more creative you will get.

In this book, we have guided and assisted you regarding how to use this software to your advantage. Starting from handling the tool box, to the different layers, photo editing, digital art, typography – you will get a detailed account of how to handle and use the software.

There are many amongst us who have an artistic bent of mind but don't know how to edit the images and hence depend on the professionals to get the work done. In the process, they end up investing a huge amount of money. But once you install Adobe Photoshop in your computer you will not have to visit a professional any more. You can easily edit the images the way you want it and that too from the comforts of your home. All that you need to do is save the image in a JPEG format and take as many printouts as you want and in different sizes as well. Always sue a high quality image with a higher resolution so that no matter how you zoom in to edit the image it does get pixelerated.

www.ingramcontent.com/pod-product-compliance
Lightning Source LLC
Chambersburg PA
CBHW071007180526
45168CB00003B/1318